MW00990265

How to Give a Bible Study

Suggestions for finding Bible study interests
—————————— AND ——————————
effective tips for leading them to Christ

Kurt Johnson

Pacific Press® Publishing Association
Nampa, Idaho
Oshawa, Ontario, Canada
www.pacificpress.com

Cover design by Michelle C. Petz
Inside design by Steve Lanto

Printed in the United States of America

Unless otherwise noted, all Scripture quotations are taken from the
New King James Version of the Bible, © 1979, 1980, 1982,
Thomas Nelson, Inc., Publishers. Used by permission.

Additional copies of this book are available by calling
toll free 1-800-765-6955 or by visiting
http://www.Adventistbookcenter.com

Library of Congress Cataloging-in-Publication Data

Johnson, Kurt W., 1950-
How to give a Bible study : suggestions for finding Bible study
interests and effective tips for leading them to Christ / Kurt
Johnson.
p. cm.
ISBN 978-0-8163-2230-5 (stitched paper back)
1. Bible--Study and teaching. I. Title.
BS600.3.J63 2007
220.071--dc22

2007022681

07 08 09 10 11 · 5 4 3 2 1

Acknowledgments

A booklet of this type is not the product of just one person. The principles for giving Bible studies have been passed down from person to person and generation to generation. Yet each individual and each generation must adapt these methods and approaches to specific cultures, times, and situations. I have shared my ideas and personal experiences in these pages, but I am indebted to others who have gone before me—as well as to various printed materials—including the following:

Mark and Ernestine Finley, *Light Your World for God* (Hart Research Center) as well as their lectures on prayer, soul winning, and giving Bible studies.

Don and Marjorie Gray's lectures, handouts, and booklets.

Carl Hobson, who took me visiting door-to-door and taught me how to give Bible studies during my first year in pastoral ministry.

E. Lonnie Melashenko, author of *What the Bible Says About . . .* (Pacific Press® Publishing Association).

He also provided invaluable editing and content suggestions.

Philip G. Samaan, *Christ's Way of Reaching People* (Review and Herald® Publishing Association).

Calvin Smith, *Giving Bible Studies* (General Conference of Seventh-day Adventists [Silver Spring, Md.: General Conference of Seventh-day Adventists]).

Training Light Bearers (Review and Herald® Publishing Association).

Ellen G. White. Many of her books provided valuable quotations; *The Great Controversy*—especially the chapter "The Waldenses"—proved particularly helpful.

Contents

Chapter 1

Yes, You Can Give a Bible Study

On a hot, sticky August afternoon I found myself standing on a sidewalk in Pasco, Washington, with my heart beating like a hammer in my chest. I was sixteen years old and facing giving my first Bible study! The prospect scared me to death. I stood there wondering, *Why in the world am I doing this?*

Actually, it was my pastor's fault. I had been baptized eight weeks earlier, and I was convicted that I needed to witness—to share my love for Jesus with others. The problem was I had no idea how to do it.

So I had made an appointment with Pastor Ralph and shared my dilemma. He immediately picked up something he called a "Gift Bible" from the corner of his desk. The plan was simple, he explained. I was to walk down the street, knock on a door, and tell the person who answered that if he completed the full set of lessons, the Bible was his to keep. I would return each week with a new lesson, and we would discuss the one I had left the week before—which presumably the person had studied, filling in the answer sheet.

Simple.

For the pastor maybe! But he was talking to Mr. Shy, a teenager who sat in the corner and trembled at the prospect of standing up in front to talk to people. That was me—the kid with the shaky voice. Now, of course there are many other ways that a sixteen-year-old can share his faith. Walking around a neighborhood, trying to give Bible studies, is probably far from the top of that list for most teens. But I believe God impressed Pastor Ralph to share with me what he did.

Why? Because that little speech launched me on a lifetime of giving Bible studies and teaching others how to share the message of the Bible with their friends and neighbors.

But that's getting way ahead of my story. Back then, a few days after my meeting with the pastor, I stood on the sidewalk in Pasco, clutching a set of lessons and a sweat-covered Bible—yes, my hands were dripping wet! If Pastor Ralph said this is what it meant to witness, then it must be God's plan for every member. I *had* to do this. I had no choice; I must obey God. What I didn't find out until much later was that I was one of only a handful of people in my church doing this!

With a trembling hand, quivering legs, and a shaky voice, I knocked on thirty doors. Most people were polite, but they declined my offer as I stared at them with a "deer in the headlights" look on my face. But finally, Patricia opened the door. Patricia—Pat, I came to call her—was a young woman in her twenties, and she said, "Sure, I'd like to study the Bible." I left Pat the first lesson and the Gift Bible, and then set an appointment to come back the next week.

What a huge relief! As I left Pat's house, I kept thinking, *Thank You, Jesus. Thank You. I've got a Bible study; no more knocking on doors!* My feet barely touched the pavement as I hurried home. God had led me to someone with whom I could share my love for the Bible.

I have to admit that when I first started giving Bible studies and visiting people who were interested in the Bible, I began the hard way. No one really showed me what to do or helped me know what to say. No one gave me a book about witnessing to read. No one took me with them to hold a Bible study to show me how it was done. I didn't even know enough to ask for help. I didn't know what questions to ask or how to lead a person to make a decision about what he was studying. I just prayed and walked down the street, Bible lessons in hand. Later, I was able to attend some training sessions. I went visiting with experienced church members and pastors. And I learned rather quickly because I had struggled so much on my own. But there is an easier way to learn to study the Bible with others.

This booklet is designed to help you get started, to help you give that first Bible study. And even if you are "seasoned" in studying the Bible with others, perhaps you will pick up some practical ideas that will strengthen your ministry. One thing I have learned through the years is that, although there are certain basic principles that apply to all Bible study situations, there is more than one approach to accomplishing the task. So if you say or do something different from what I suggest in this booklet, that's OK—work in your own armor. What really matters is that you and I, together with God, are a team leading people to the foot of the cross and on to eternal life.

My experience as a sixteen-year-old did teach me one important thing—anyone can give a Bible study. Yes, anyone—even you! It might be hard at first, but with God's help you can give a Bible study or be a partner with someone else who leads out in the study. You may be saying to yourself, "Pastor Kurt, you don't know me! Giving Bible studies just isn't my gift."

Well, that's exactly how I felt when I started back there in Pasco, Washington. But today, giving people Bible studies is one of the greatest joys of my life. So keep on reading, and let's journey together.

Chapter 2

But I'm "Only"
a Lay Person

They made tents for a living. They also loved Jesus and gave Bible studies. We can read about them in Acts 18. Aquilla and his wife, Priscilla, were Jews who had moved from Italy to the Greek city of Corinth. Upon their arrival they established a business—making tents—and when the apostle Paul arrived from Athens and began ministering to the Christians in Corinth, they invited him to work with them in their shop.

Now the three spent quite a bit of time together. And I'm sure as they cut and sewed fabric into tents, these two lay people discussed with the great apostle various aspects of sharing the gospel. In fact, it seems that these two tent-makers got so excited about Jesus and His transforming power that they began sharing with others at every opportunity. The Bible tells us about Aquilla and Priscilla ministering in Ephesus.

We read in Acts 18:24 that a Jew named Apollos, "an eloquent man and mighty in the Scriptures," arrived in Ephesus. This man had been instructed in the way of the Lord; "and being fervent in spirit, he spoke and taught accurately the things of the Lord, though he knew only the baptism of John" (verse 25).

Aquilla and Priscilla heard Apollos speaking "boldly" to the people. But they soon realized that his understanding of the Scriptures left something to be desired. So they had a Bible study with Apollos "and explained to him the way of God more accurately." Verse 26 states that they took him "aside." In other words, they met with him privately. The three believers sat down together and had a Bible study together.

It would be interesting to have listened in on that discussion! What we do know is that Apollos proved to be teachable. He profited from the study. When this gifted man left Corinth and went to Achaia, he greatly helped the believers there and "vigorously" gave a Bible study on the topic of Jesus as the Messiah (see verses 27, 28). As we look at this account, we can see that Aquilla and Priscilla demonstrated several characteristics that enabled them to be effective in giving a Bible study.

1. As lay people, they were committed members of a local church.
2. They studied the Bible personally; they understood the Scriptures.
3. They were willing learners and committed to service for God.
4. They looked for opportunities to talk to others about the Bible.

5. They must have been humble, gracious, kind, and tactful. (Otherwise a dynamic man like Apollos would have been upset at their attempts to correct his views!)
6. They stepped out in faith and depended on the Holy Spirit.

The experience of Aquilla and Priscilla suggests a series of questions to ask yourself. If you can answer "yes" to the following questions, then you can be part of a team of two that gives a Bible study. Yes, even you!

1. Are you a follower of Jesus?
2. Do you study your Bible and pray regularly?
3. Are you willing to learn new things?
4. Are you open to looking for opportunities to share your love for Jesus and the truth of the Bible with others?
5. Do you desire, by God's grace, to be humble, kind, gracious, and caring to others?
6. Do you trust God and desire to grow daily in your dependence on Him for strength and power through the Holy Spirit?

If you answered "yes" to these questions or if you can say "That is my desire, with God's help," then you can give a Bible study. And remember, when you get involved in sharing the message of the Bible with others, you join a wonderful group of Christians down through the centuries who have experienced the joy and blessing of helping make the Word come alive for others.

Have you ever heard of a group called the "Bereans"? They're mentioned in Acts 17:10–12. When Paul and Silas first spoke to them about the Scriptures, the Bereans immediately began to search the Bible to improve their understanding. They became known as models of open-minded study of the Word. I like how the Bible describes their study habits: "They received the word with all readiness, and searched the Scriptures daily to find out whether these things were so. Therefore many of them believed" (Acts 17:11, 12). Not only did they believe, they also shared what they learned.

So did the Waldenses, a persecuted group of faithful Christian believers in medieval Europe who had to seek refuge in the caves and lofty peaks of the Alps. As children, Waldensian boys and girls memorized large portions of the Scriptures. Their pastors and lay members chose trades or professions that gave them an opportunity to witness. Many became peddlers, selling various wares so that they could meet a lot of people and look for opportunities to share the Bible. At a time when access to the Word was quite restricted, the Waldenses shared precious Bible passages either by word of mouth or through carefully hand-copied portions of the Word.

The Waldenses were trained to be careful in avoiding persecution from hostile authorities. But they also learned to be bold, always eager for opportunities to share God's Word as the Spirit led them. Their love for the Bible and their passion for sharing what they learned stood out dramatically in a very dark age. So they did suffer persecution. But their sole purpose in life continued to be lifting up Jesus to a world in need of a Savior.

In the Seventh-day Adventist Church a revival atmosphere prevailed in the late 1800s. It generated something of a let's-give-a-Bible-study movement. The movement got its start at a California camp meeting. Prior to that event, Adventists presented scriptural truths to the general public usually through preaching and by sharing literature. Some church members were involved in studying the Bible personally with others, but no coordinated plan existed for that kind of outreach.

But then in 1882 something happened in California, in what was supposed to be the land of beaches, warm climate, year-around flowers, and nonstop sunshine. Some of the worst storms in history collided with the week of camp meeting. There were heavy rains, mud slides, floods, and destruction.

As keynote speaker S. N. Haskell began to preach, heavy clouds and a downpour of rain greeted his words. In the middle of his sermon, thunder rocked the campground, and lightning lit up the midday sky. In this day before microphones, no one could hear the preacher. Without missing a beat, Pastor Haskell walked to the center of the tent. He told everyone to gather around him as close as possible.

Instead of continuing to preach, he took the topic of his sermon and assigned the members of the audience Bible verses to read out loud from their Bibles. He then asked a question and had an individual read the text. Sometimes he made a comment, but generally questions that arose were answered directly from the Bible.

The audience loved this approach! Ellen White was not at the service, but her son Willie (Pastor W. C. White) gave his mother a glowing report. At a meeting the next day she said that what had taken place was God's plan for the church. She would later write, "The plan of holding Bible readings was a heaven-born idea" (*Gospel Workers*, p. 192). Ellen White asserted that God wanted thousands of Adventists going door-to-door with their Bibles teaching the Scriptures in this manner. Here is what she wrote: "Hundreds and thousands were seen visiting families, and opening before them the word of God. . . . On every side doors were thrown open to the proclamation of the truth. The world seemed to be lightened with the heavenly influence" (*Testimonies for the Church*, vol. 9, p. 126).

A resolution was passed at the camp meeting that a plan be put in place to teach church members how to present a "Bible reading," the purpose being to "better inform themselves in the Scriptures," and also of "interesting their neighbors" in "the special truths for these last days" (*Signs of the Times*, September 27, 1883).

Following up on this resolution, Pastor Haskell wrote a set of Bible lessons—questions with Scripture answers—and a ten-day training institute was organized in October of the same year. The announcement for the institute read, "Not only young men and women are wanted, but men of mature years; even if their heads are sprinkled with gray hairs, they are none too old to visit families and tell what God has done for them, and read the Scriptures" (ibid., October 18, 1883).

Adventist colleges immediately began to include courses on how to give Bible studies. Training centers sprang up in churches and large cities. Students and adults spent weekends and summer vacations learning from experienced instructors how to make a visit, meet needs, answer questions, present a Bible study, and secure decisions. They learned about the basics involved in what was known as "the art of giving Bible studies," defined as one important phase of the "highest of all sciences"—the "science of soul-winning." In addition, a collection of studies were assembled in a book called *Bible Readings for the Home.*

What took place in these first Bible readings or Bible studies, as we call them today? In an article he wrote for *Signs of the Times*, August 14, 1884, Pastor Haskell recounted the following successes that people had regarding Bible studies:

- They held Bible readings in the homes of families.

- They obtained subscriptions to *Signs* magazine.
- Families invited their neighbors.
- Five to fifteen persons were attending the Bible readings.
- They sat around a large table.
- Each person had his or her own Bible.
- Each person looked up the different Bible texts.
- Members needed to be instructed on how to give a Bible study successfully.
- Some had a natural ability to give Bible studies; others needed to follow a specific plan.

In addition, a special monthly magazine, the *Bible-Reading Gazette*, was developed for these new "lay Bible workers." The magazine included testimonies, "how-to" instruction, resources, and spiritual guidance.

As you can see, leading out in a Bible study—with one person or a small group of people—is a simple, God-led plan, rooted in the history of the Advent movement.

So, what qualifies someone to give a Bible study to another person? It simply takes a person who loves Jesus. It simply takes a committed heart and a desire to tell friends and family about Jesus and the message of the Bible. It's a choice—a choice to become involved. Do you want to get involved in giving Bible studies and be as effective as possible? If so, the next few pages will help you get started.

Chapter 3

Prayer and Soul Winning

"Young man, make up your mind! Either start working or get out of town!" That's what a policeman told Philip, a college classmate and friend of mine. Philip was a sophomore in college; he was trying to sell Christian books door-to-door to earn money for tuition. But he was so scared he couldn't get out of his car. So he drove up and down the main street of a small Idaho town. Several townspeople became suspicious and called the police. So Philip had to explain to the officer what he was doing, confessing his nervousness and fear. The officer's emphatic command—either get to work or leave town—drove Philip back to his hotel room. There on his knees he talked to God about his dilemma.

Philip prayed and prayed some more. He tried to focus on the words of promise in Isaiah 41:10,

"Fear not, for I am with you;
Be not dismayed, for I am your God.

I will strengthen you,
Yes, I will help you,
I will uphold you with My righteous right
 hand."

At last, Philip decided to claim that promise for himself and begin knocking on doors.

Philip learned a valuable lesson that summer. *Prayer and soul winning go together!*

In fact, here's an essential principle: Prayer is the number one priority in giving a Bible study.

If you want to be a witness for Jesus Christ, your first task is to become a man or woman of prayer—a boy or girl of prayer. Nothing is more important. The simple fact is that if you can pray, God can use you to lead people to Jesus. There are two main reasons to pray if you want to witness for Jesus:

- First, prayer is the antidote to fear. Prayer and claiming the promises of God's Word is the path to becoming a confident, Spirit-filled Christian. Prayer helps us to be more like Jesus. Prayer empowers us for ministry.
- Second, you access the power of the Holy Spirit through prayer—and only the Holy Spirit can enlighten and change the lives of those you are studying with.

As my friends Mark and Ernestine Finley often assert, "In the work of soul winning, there is no substitute for prayer." Let's think for a moment about this Bible promise from the apostle John: "Now this is the confidence that we have in Him, that if we ask anything according to His will, He hears us. And if we know that He hears us, whatever we ask, we know that we have the petitions that we have asked of Him" (1 John 5:14, 15).

This promise contains the two ingredients that are essential to leading people to Jesus. What are these two ingredients?

1. Prayer (". . . if we ask anything . . .") and
2. Faith (". . . we know that we have the petitions that we have asked . . . ")

Now, it's possible—without prayer—to convince a person intellectually that the truths in the Bible are correct. Without prayer, you can even influence a person's behavior to some extent. But you can never win a person to Jesus—bring him or her to accept Jesus as Savior and Lord—without prayer. Conversion is a *miracle.* Conversion isn't a human accomplishment; it's a direct result of the work of the Holy Spirit.

Ellen White wrote, "Prayer and faith will do what no power on earth can accomplish" (*The Ministry of Healing*, p. 509). That's something to think about! The greatest power on this earth is not the power exercised by a president or prime minister or some other world leader. It's not a nuclear weapon. It's not all the funds hidden away in Swiss bank accounts. The greatest power on earth is the power contained in the life, death, and resurrection of the Lord Jesus Christ. And prayer and faith make that power available to each one of us! Why not reach out and accept it?

Do you want to overcome your fear of sharing Jesus with others? (I know you do!) Do you want to have a part of bringing someone to accept Jesus? (I know that your answer is "yes.") Then *pray in faith,* believing that God has already fulfilled your desire.

Here are four more reasons we should pray for people as we share Jesus with them.

1. Prayer enables God to speak to us personally about issues in our life, about sins that may be hindering us from successful soul winning. The Bible declares that "all have sinned and fall short of the glory of God" (Romans 3:23). Paul admits in Romans 7:19, "For the good that I will to do, I do not do; but the evil I will not to do, that I practice." Prayer connects us to Jesus Christ, the source of victory. Jesus is the One who forgives us, cleanses us, and empowers us to overcome sin.

2. Prayer deepens our desire for the things we pray about. When you pray for your son or daughter, for your neighbor, or for your Bible study student, these individuals become a priority in your life. You begin to look more keenly for ways to meet their needs.

3. Prayer puts us in touch with divine wisdom. Most of us feel very inadequate when it comes to sharing the message about Jesus with others. And it's true—as humans we *are* inadequate. But Jesus has promised to give us the kind of wisdom that comes directly from Him. I like that, don't you? Two scriptures anchor this point:

> If any of you lacks wisdom, let him ask of God, who gives to all liberally and without reproach, and it will be given to him (James 1:5).

> "The Lord GOD has given Me
> The tongue of the learned,
> That I should know how to speak
> A word in season to him who is weary"
> (Isaiah 50:4).

4. Prayer enables God to work more powerfully than He could if we did not pray. Ellen White wrote, "It is a part of God's plan to grant us, in answer to the prayer of faith, that which He would not bestow did we not thus ask" (*The Great Controversy,* p. 525). Think about this statement for a moment. God freely bestows many blessings on human beings. But apparently, there are some things that God will not give unless we ask for them. Why? I believe there are two reasons: (1) God wants us to acknowledge that He is the Giver of all things, and (2) God wants us to choose freely. He wants our permission to act in our life or in the life of another. God will not force Himself upon anyone.

Never forget, the number one priority in Bible study ministry is prayer.

So, first of all, develop a prayer list of those you're studying with—or those whom you would like to interest in Bible study. Be specific in your requests as you pray for these persons:

> "Oh, that one might plead for a man with
> God,
> As a man pleads for his neighbor!" (Job
> 16:21).

> "Moreover, as for me, far be it from me that I should sin against the Lord in ceasing to pray for you; but I will teach you the good and the right way" (1 Samuel 12:23).

Pray alone; make your petitions a conscious request between you and God. Also pray with other Christians; invoke the power of God's promise that He is present where two or more are gathered together in His name (see Matthew 18:20). Never forget: Prayer activates the greatest power on earth.

As Christians, we discuss and study the best means and methods of sharing Jesus with others. That's a good thing. But never forget that *only God can convert the heart.* When we become people of prayer, we unleash more of God's power in leading people to Himself. It's interesting to note that Scripture does not tell us to "organize" always or to "equip" always or to "preach" always or to "attend committees" always. But it does tell us to "pray" always (see 1 Thessalonians 5:17).

The greatest gift a Christian has to offer the church, family and friends, Bible students, and the whole world is the gift of his or her personal prayer life.

Chapter 4

How to Find Bible Study Students

Do you remember my opening story and how I knocked on about thirty doors just to find someone with whom to study the Bible? I have learned a few things since then. Now, each day I ask God to give me what I call "sharing-my-faith" eyes. I keep my eyes open for people who might be receptive to an invitation to study the Bible. I've found that people fall into three basic categories when it comes to Bible studies: (1) those who request Bible studies, (2) those who don't ask for Bible studies but who will say "yes" if asked, and (3) those who are not yet ready to study the Bible. The key is to zero in on the first two groups. It's a little like picking fruit when it's ripe.

When I was fifteen years old I lived in Yuma, Arizona. I tried to earn some money by picking lemons. During my first day on the job I felt about as useful as a penguin in the Sahara. The twelve-foot ladder weighed almost more than I did, and I had to try to balance a full bag of lemons from my shoulder as I climbed down! My boss handed me a wire ring gauge and said, "Don't pick all of the lemons hanging on a tree. Look at the color and make sure the lemon is too large to fit through this ring gauge. If a lemon is green or too small, leave it on the tree, and we'll pick it later."

The first few days it seemed to take forever—like trying to get frozen water through a pipe—just to decide which lemons were right to pick. But soon my "lemon picking eyes" got better. Eventually I threw away the wire gauge ring because I could tell right away which lemons were right for picking. I've found it works the same way with people. God will help you find ripe fruit, people open to His Word.

One thing you can count on: When you ask God to give you "sharing-your-faith" eyes, He will! Why? Because part of His plan for your life is to have you tell others the story of Jesus.

In fact, Jesus gave us an important clue about where to look for Bible study students. Just before He returned to heaven He told His disciples, " 'But you shall receive power when the Holy Spirit has come upon you; and you shall be witnesses to Me in Jerusalem, and in all Judea and Samaria, and to the end of the earth' " (Acts 1:8).

For the apostles, Jerusalem was home. Judea and Samaria were nearby, but essentially outside their "city limits." And beyond Judea and Samaria was—the entire world! So the first step in becoming a "witness" is simply this: Begin in the town where you live. Make a list of all the people near you who might respond to an invitation to study the Bible:

- your immediate family and other relatives
- your neighbors and the people you work with
- people you meet every day—store clerks, gas station attendants, mail carriers, receptionists, hair dressers, etc.
- people who are served by the Community Services of your local church
- people who attend your church's Community Services programs, such as cooking classes, healthful living classes, or grief recovery seminars
- visitors to your church
- people attending evangelistic reaping meetings
- people who are listening to or watching Adventist radio and television ministries
- former and nonattending church members
- people who have purchased books from a literature evangelist
- students of correspondence Bible schools
- readers of *Signs of the Times*, *Message,* and *El Centinela* magazines.

Remember, anyone can be a friend. Neighborliness costs nothing and is one of the most effective outreach tools.

Now let's focus on some specific ways you can develop "sharing-your-faith" eyes. Here is how it works.

1. Pray every day and ask God to bring you someone that day whom you can point to Him. Planting a gospel seed can happen through a brief comment or a more extended spiritual conversation. When you pray daily for an opportunity to share Jesus, God will help you recognize opportunities.

2. Watch for conversational contacts. Suppose someone at the hair salon or the grocery store makes a comment about a destructive hurricane or tornado that has been in the news. You might respond by saying something like, "Isn't it terrible? I really feel sorry for those people, and I pray for them. I know that faith is often what pulls people through a tragedy like that."

Recently, I met Rene, who told me about the fruitful conversations she has had with various individuals. Rene makes it a habit to talk about her spiritual life in a natural way whenever the opportunity arises, and she often finds people who respond positively to her. She's not preachy or overbearing. But she's not embarrassed to talk about her life either. She says, "I just drop simple things into the conversation. Things such as, 'I went shopping with a friend of mine from church, and we had a great time together!' Or 'I spent last Sabbath afternoon hiking with my family near a waterfall.' " Do you see what Rene is doing? Her simple, natural comments are planting seeds that can develop, then or later, into deeper conversations about spiritual themes.

3. Share a book, a pamphlet, a magazine, or a video/DVD. When someone shows interest in a particular topic—parenting, coping with grief, raising children, health, prophecy, a biblical issue—be prepared to tell them about a booklet, a magazine, or a DVD that helped you with answers on this subject. Be prepared to give or loan them the resource. This may lead to a discussion later regarding God, the Bible, and spiritual themes. It may even open up an opportunity to share a Bible study guide with this person. (I like to call these lessons "Bible *reading* guides" rather than "*study* guides" since many people feel they have had quite enough of *studying* while they were in school.)

4. Meet needs and be present when people are hurting or celebrating. When someone has a baby, celebrates a birthday, gets a promotion, has surgery, or mourns a loss, write that person a note in a card, give a gift, or prepare a dish of food. In other words, be there for that person at this important time. Pray for and with him or her when it is appropriate. Loan a helpful booklet.

5. Distribute Bible course enrollment cards. This is a simple way to get requests from people for Bible studies. An enrollment card is a postcard that offers free Bible study guides if a person simply mails the card. You can put your local church's post office box on the card or use the address of the Voice of Prophecy Bible Correspondence School. You can distribute these enrollment cards door-to-door in your neighborhood.

You can mail enrollment cards to those who have visited your church or expressed an interest in spiritual themes. Or you can mail cards in bulk to the residents of your town or to selected ZIP codes or postal codes.

Those who respond by mailing the card are *specifically requesting Bible study guides.* So when you visit these individuals, you are going *at their request!* That makes it easier.

Here is an excellent plan that some churches follow. Each week during the Sabbath School class, teachers hand out Bible study enrollment cards and encourage every class member to take at least one card and do something with it during the next week—hand it to someone, include it in the envelope when paying a bill, leave it on the seat of a bus, subway train, or airplane, etc. Business owners can keep a stack of cards at their places of business. There are many different ways to distribute these cards.

Several years ago, Fred found a Bible study enrollment card in the dumpster of his daughter's apartment in Virginia. He mailed the card to the address given, which was the local church's post office box. Today, Fred is attending church and following Jesus. As long as the card is somewhere in view, God can use it. God can use a card even when it is in the garbage can!

Bible study enrollment cards are one of the most effective—and yet inexpensive—ways to connect with people who are interested in studying the Bible.

I hope this encouraging comment from Ellen White will help you get started finding and studying with those who are receptive.

Wherever you can gain access to the people by the fireside, improve your opportunity. Take your Bible, and open before them its great truths. Your success will not depend so much upon your knowledge and accomplishments, as upon your ability to find your way to the heart. By being social and coming close to the people, you may turn the current of their thoughts more readily than by the most able discourse. The presentation of Christ in the family, by the fireside, and in small gatherings in private houses, is often more successful in winning souls to Jesus than are sermons delivered in the open air, to the moving throng, or even in halls or churches (*Gospel Workers,* p. 193).

Chapter 5

Preparing the Bible Study

Step #1. Pray. Surrender your life and ministry to God. Ask Him to cleanse your life of all sin, to change you by His power so that you will be like Jesus. Ask God to give you a passion for souls like Jesus had. Ask Him for wisdom and insight as you prepare to lead out in the Bible study. Pray for your students; pray that God will work through you in meeting their needs.

Step #2. Believe. Believe that God will use you and give you success. Remember, Satan will try to disrupt your study. So when difficulties arise, don't give up. Don't give the enemy the upper hand. Pray instead. Claim God's promises. Ask for wisdom. Ask God to bind Satan and his angels. As the songwriter says, "Never give up . . ." Jesus has already won the victory over Satan. Claim the promise. Believe the promise. And live the promise.

Step #3. Witness about Jesus. Your purpose as you study the Bible with others is to witness about Jesus (see Acts 1:8). As my friend Calvin Smith observes, "When you study the Bible with someone, your aim isn't merely to present facts. It isn't just to give Bible studies. Your aim must be *to lead souls to Christ.* Your purpose is not to convince the *mind* that you have the truth about the day, the diet, and death. It is to awaken a *heart* response and commitment to a living personal Savior, seven days a week, as the answer to every need. Our points of faith are important only as one knows and accepts Jesus as Savior and Lord. Christ must be seen as the *center* of every doctrine."

Step #4. Study and complete each lesson yourself. Look up the texts. Write the answers in the blanks. This will help you become familiar with the material you will be studying with your student. Look up words you can't pronounce, the meaning of a phrase; underline sentences in the lesson that you want to emphasize.

Determine what key texts you want to look up in the Bible and discuss with the students. If you had to choose only four or five texts on the topic of the lesson, which ones would you choose? If you don't know what the texts really state, it will be difficult to be adequately prepared.

In addition, I find out all the information I can find on the four or five key texts that I have chosen. I read Bible commentaries, Bible dictionaries, and other resources. (I may personally read what Ellen White has to say on a topic, but I use only the Bible to answer the questions in the lesson and when discussing it with students.)

Step #5. Make a brief outline. What thought will you use to begin the lesson? Read the introduction in the printed lesson, but also think about your first words as you study the lesson with the student. Write down key points you want to be sure to remember and discuss regarding the Bible texts you will be reading together. Familiarize yourself with the decision/commitment questions that are at the end of the study guide. These commitment questions on each topic are a crucial part of the study. Finally, plan your concluding/summarizing points and comments.

Step #6. Establish the goals and purpose of the Bible study. In order to accomplish anything, you must know what you want the outcome to be and determine what steps are necessary to accomplish that goal or purpose. This principle certainly applies to Bible study.

Your top priority must be the people with whom you are studying! Don't mistakenly assume that the presentation of the study itself is more important than the people with whom you are studying. If you overlook their personal needs and their unique circumstances—pressing on to cover the material in the lesson, no matter what—then your insensitivity will cause many to quit studying.

Every time you are in a student's home, your priorities—your goals—should be the following:

- To develop a friendship and a positive relationship with the individual or group.

- To meet, as far as possible, any personal needs that come up during the study.
- To adapt to the circumstances in the home—sickness, unexpected company, a school program, a ball game, a television program that the family wants to watch, etc. Remember, flexibility is the key to being able to keep returning and studying with this person or family. Let them see that you genuinely care about them and understand their personal situation.
- To study the Bible lesson.
- To look for an opportunity to briefly share your personal testimony.
- To look for an opportunity to lead individuals to accept Jesus as their Lord and Savior.

Of course, as you keep visiting and studying, the last two items in the list will naturally arise out of the content of the study guides as you keep visiting and studying with the student.

Step #7. Choose a Bible study/visiting partner. Jesus sent out His disciples two by two (see Mark 6:7). The advantages of having a visiting partner are many:

- The two of you serve as prayer partners for each other.
- You are able to encourage one another. "Woe to him who is alone when he falls, / For he has no one to help him up" (Ecclesiastes 4:10).

- If there are small children in the home, one of the partners can play with them or read them stories to keep them from interrupting the study.
- While one of you is talking and discussing the lesson, the other can be praying. Before the study begins, always decide which of you will lead out in the discussion. The other partner can then be ready to play a supportive role. However, both partners need to be equally prepared for the study.
- If one partner is not able to attend a study for some reason, the other partner can conduct the study. If this occurs, it's a good idea for the lone partner to take someone else along to the study. This preserves the two-by-two dynamic and also shows someone else how to give a Bible study. In addition, it acquaints the Bible student with one more persons in the church.

Before you make your initial visit to the home, consider the effect of certain scenarios. If two men knock on a woman's door, she may be intimidated or even scared. A man at home may not feel comfortable having two women visiting him. Initially, it is best for a man and a woman to visit. This can be a husband and wife or another compatible man and woman team. When you return for the second visit, you can evaluate the circumstances in the home and determine who will continue the studies.

Step #8. Let God's Word speak for itself. This is a vital point. Remember that the same Holy Spirit who inspired and guided the Bible writers is still changing the lives of those who read God's Word today. This is an extremely important concept. The success of a Bible study does not depend upon your presentation of the study—how well you do. Obviously, you want to be prepared and be as effective as you can as you study the Bible with others. But if you simply "go" in obedience to Christ's command, even if you simply have the student read the Bible texts in the lesson and do nothing else, God can still transform their lives through the power of the Holy Spirit and His Word. Even if you think you are stumbling in your presentation, God can still use you to change lives. Why? Because God's Word transforms people—not you or your presentation. Memorize these promises:

- "For Your word has given me life" (Psalm 119:50).
- " 'Sanctify them by Your truth. Your word is truth' " (John 17:17).
- "Be diligent to present yourself approved to God, a worker who does not need to be ashamed, rightly dividing the word of truth" (2 Timothy 2:15).
- "All Scripture is given by inspiration of God, and is profitable for doctrine, for reproof, for correction, for instruction in righteousness" (2 Timothy 3:16).

Notice that these texts refer to God's Word as "truth." The Bible tells us that when we bring the great and precious promises of God's Word into our lives, we partake of His divine nature (see 2 Peter 1:4). Jesus explained it this way: " 'It is written, "Man shall not live by bread alone, but by every word that proceeds from the mouth of God" ' " (Matthew 4:4).

Here is an excellent principle to follow: "The Bible is its own expositor. Scripture is to be compared with scripture" (Ellen G. White, *Counsels to Parents, Teachers, and Students,* p. 462). The Word of God is a living word. It is powerful; it affects the thoughts and intents of the heart; it is the channel through which the Holy Spirit speaks to an individual.

Let the Bible speak for itself. A student can argue with your opinion, but if he or she believes that the Bible is God's inspired Word, then it's pointless to argue with its clear statements. When the answer to a question comes from Scripture, the argument is over before it starts.

Your essential role in a Bible study is to open God's Word and make it possible for an individual to read what God is saying to him so that it can penetrate his heart and mind through the power of the Holy Spirit. The Holy Spirit is the One who awakens and convicts. It is only by God's grace that you are able to present His Word. Do so—and then watch Him act!

Chapter 6

Presenting the
Bible Study

There are two basic approaches to giving personal Bible studies—the shorter *doorstep study* method and the longer *home study* method.

In the first, the instructor simply leaves the Bible study guide with the student at the door and makes an appointment to return in a week to review the lesson with the student. During the week, before the instructor returns, the student reads the lesson on his own, looks up the Bible texts, and fills in the responses or answers called for by the study guide. When the instructor returns in a week, he reviews the student's responses, answers any questions the student may have, and makes a few comments about the lesson. Then he leaves the next lesson, making an appointment to return a week later. This process continues until the series of lessons is completed. The review of the lesson can actually be done on the student's doorstep, but of course, the goal is to review the lesson with the student in his or her home.

In the longer home study method, the instructor and the student sit down together in the home. Together, they go through the lesson, looking up the Bible texts and completing the answers called for.

Either method of study can be effective, and the specific process of studying the lesson is quite similar with both methods. Whether you are following the doorstep method or studying the lessons together with the student in the home, the following principles apply.

First contact with the student

When you go to the home of the person with whom you hope to begin studies, you should take several things with you. If possible, bring the actual card the person mailed requesting studies. Sometimes people forget having mailed the request, and the card will help them recall having asked for Bible studies. (Keep the information from the card—name, address, etc.— in a master file as well.)

Also be sure you have a number of Bibles in your car in case the student does not own a Bible. And have several copies of the first lesson in the series and Bible correspondence course enrollment cards. You may find other family members who also want to study the Bible, so you'll need several copies of the first lesson. And if the person or other family members don't want to actually study the Bible in their home with an instructor, they may be interested in taking a correspondence Bible course by mail. If this is the case, have them fill in the card and tell them you will enroll them in a course they can complete by mail.

Knocking on the door

When you arrive and the student opens the door, he will have three questions you will need to answer immediately. He may not ask these questions out loud, but they will be in his mind nevertheless:

- Who are you?
- What do you want?
- How long are you going to stay?

Here's a sample of what you might say when the student comes to the door. "Hi! I'm Kurt Johnson, and this is Bill Smith [point to your partner]. Are you Sam Jones? You mailed this card requesting free Bible lessons [show him the card], and we've stopped by to bring you the first study guide. Do you have a few minutes for us to explain how you can get started with this first Bible guide?"

Notice how you have answered all three of the questions that are in the person's mind; you have told him who you are, why you are at his door, and how much of his time you want. At this point the person may invite you in or he may not. Be prepared for either response. If the person doesn't ask you to come inside, simply continue the conversation at the door. "Sam, I'm sure you'll enjoy these Bible guides. They are simple to complete and very informative. [Hold the first study guide in your hand and show it to him.] Here is how it works. You read the brief introduction to the lesson. Read the questions and look up the Bible texts. Then write your answers in the blanks provided. Once you've completed filling out each answer, there is a question at the end of the lesson for you to record your response to the lesson. I'd like to come back in a week. I'll complete the study guide too. We can review our responses together, and I'll give you the next study guide. We'll follow this procedure each week until you've completed the set of study guides. Does this sound OK to you?"

If the person says yes, then set up an appointment for the next week. If he hesitates, ask if he needs more time than one week. If he still hesitates or if he says, "I thought the lessons would come in the mail," tell him that he can indeed study the lessons by mail. If that is his preference, make sure you have his correct mailing information. If necessary, have him fill out an enrollment card for the correspondence course. Take the card with you and mail it to the Voice of Prophecy Correspondence Bible School. Or even better, set up a Discover Bible School in your own local church and be this person's Bible instructor by mail. (Contact the Voice of Prophecy for information on how to set up a Discover Bible School operated by your local church.)

If the person agrees to have you return in a week to review the lesson with him, ask if he has a Bible. If not, give him one. Many people are not familiar with how to find texts in the Bible, and this can be a problem. Some Bible study guides give both the usual text reference

(Bible book, chapter, and verse) and also the page number in a particular edition of the Bible where that text appears. This makes it much easier for many students to find the texts in the Bible. But if the lessons and the Bibles you are using are not paginated together, and if the student is not familiar with finding Bible texts, you will need to study the lessons together with him or use study guides that actually have the Bible text printed in the lesson for each question.

The second visit

When you return for the second visit, bring extra copies of the first lesson in case the student has lost the study guide you left a week earlier—or in case additional family members or friends want to take part in the study. Be sure to bring with you the completed copy of the first lesson that you have personally studied, with the answers filled in by yourself.

Go in faith, believing that God is with you. I like this encouraging promise: "Workers for Christ are never to think, much less to speak, of failure in their work. The Lord Jesus is our efficiency in all things" (Ellen G. White, *Gospel Workers*, p. 19).

Knock on the door. When the student, Sam, comes to the door, say, "Hi, Sam. How are you doing this afternoon? Bill and I have come back today, as we promised, to review your study guide with you." (Usually, Sam will invite you to come in. If not, go ahead and do a brief review of the lesson at the door.) Leave the second lesson. By the third visit, Sam will likely invite you inside. If not, and if you sense that he is becoming comfortable with you, ask, "May I come in for a few minutes?"

Once you are seated in the home, make everyone comfortable by saying, "How was your week, Sam?" Spend a few minutes simply getting acquainted. Then say, "Sam, did you enjoy your study guide this week? Did you learn anything new?"

Conducting the study

After he has time to respond, take out your completed study guide and say, "Let's review our answers together." Follow these steps:

1. Begin with a short prayer. "Our Father, we ask that as we study together, You will guide us by the Holy Spirit. Help us understand our topic today. We ask this in the name of Jesus, Amen."

2. Read the introduction to the lesson.

3. Explain how you will review the lessons. Say something like this: "I've completed the lesson, too. Maybe it would be easiest if I read the questions, and then you can share your answers and we'll talk about them."

If more than one student is involved in the study, say, "If any of you have a different answer as we review the lesson, let us know, and we'll read the Bible text again to clarify the answer. It's OK if our answers are different. We all get different answers sometimes. We'll just look up the Bible text and see what the Bible says. This is a learning experience." Have the students take turns giving their answers.

4. If someone has a wrong answer never say, "That answer is wrong." Instead, say, "We seem to have different thoughts [responses] to this question. Let's read the Bible text again and see if we can determine the answer together from the Bible."

Usually, the student with the wrong answer will spot his mistake right away. If not, you may need to read the question and say, "What words in the Bible text answer the question?"

Make sure the student has written an answer for each question—not just copying the entire Bible text into the blank. If they are simply reproducing the Bible text, they may not actually understand the question or the answer. If the student's answer is correct, say, "That's good!" Or "That's excellent!" Let your students know that you are a learner, too. Do not come across as the authority on the topic; such an attitude will stifle discussion and interaction.

5. Remember to be kind and tactful during the study. Use a gentle, understanding tone of voice. Ellen White wrote, "The tones of the voice have much to do in affecting the hearts of those that hear" (*Testimonies for the Church,* vol. 2, p. 615). She was referring to preaching, but the principle applies equally to our general conversations as well.

So if a student has written an incorrect answer, you can say—in a kindly tone of voice—"We seem to have different thoughts [answers] about that question. Let's check the Bible verse together again." Always be encouraging. Once you finish reviewing the lesson together and the student has done his best, write "very good" or "excellent" on his study guide. Never write "fair" or "poor." After all, it's an excellent thing just to be willing to study God's Word!

6. *Be a good listener and ask questions.* As you review the questions and answers in the lesson, frequently ask questions such as, "Is the text clear to you?" "That word or phrase is a little difficult; do you understand what it means?" "Is the topic clear to you?" "Do you have questions?" "Do you want more information?"

7. *Tactfully postpone answering questions that will be covered in a future study guide.* The lessons are designed to build a biblical foundation from lesson to lesson so that the student will be prepared to understand more difficult topics when they are presented. If you attempt to answer a question on a topic before the student is able to understand the biblical basis for the answer, it may actually stifle his interest. For example, the topic of the Sabbath or heaven may have little meaning to a student who hasn't yet accepted Jesus as his Savior and the Lord of every area of his life. If the student asks a question that he is not yet prepared for, say, "That's an excellent question. We'll be studying that entire topic in a later lesson in a few weeks. Is it OK if we wait until then to answer your question?"

If the student doesn't seem satisfied to wait, give a brief answer, commenting, "We'll look at this in more detail in a few weeks." For example, if the student asks, "Why do you go to church on Saturday?" and he isn't satisfied when you suggest holding that question until you reach that topic in the lessons, you might briefly reply, "We go to church on Saturday based on the fourth commandment found in Exodus chapter twenty, verse eight. It says that the seventh day is the Sabbath. The Bible has a lot to say about this topic, and we'll be looking at it in depth in a few weeks. But thanks for your question."

8. *Don't be embarrassed if the student asks you a question you can't answer.* No one knows the answer to every question. If the student asks you a question for which you don't know the answer, simply say, "That's a good question. I'll look up what the Bible says about that, and we can examine the answer from the Bible next week."

9. *Encourage the student if he hasn't completed the study guide when you return.* There are numerous reasons why the student may not have completed the study guide. He may not know how to find the Bible texts. He may not be interested. The questions may have seemed too hard. The student may have gotten busy. Or he may simply have forgotten. Whatever the reason, you will need to help him get started. Say something like, "If you have a few minutes we can begin the study guide together right now. Do you have a few minutes?"

If he says yes and invites you into the home, then answer the first few questions with him. Then say, "Now that we have part of the guide completed, you can complete the rest of the guide yourself for next week." If he wants you to complete the entire study guide with him, then do so.

If the student says he has changed his mind and isn't interested in completing the study guide—or if he says he is too busy to have you continue coming to his home—say, "I understand. I know how busy life can be. Let me give you my phone number in case your schedule lightens up." (Write the number on the top of the study guide). Continue by saying, "Also, you can study the guides by correspondence. Would you like to study by mail?" (If the student responds positively, then sign him up for Voice of Prophecy correspondence lessons through your local church or the Voice of Prophecy Correspondence Bible School.)

Some additional tips for effective Bible studies

1. Make Jesus the central theme of each Bible study.

2. In the first few lessons your goal is to introduce the student to Jesus and to give him an opportunity to accept Jesus as his Lord and Savior. If he hasn't accepted Jesus into his life, then the Bible messages will not be as relevant to him as they would be otherwise. The student will not see any reason to accept the subjects he is studying. Doctrines have meaning and significance only when viewed through the Cross.

3. Keep the Bible study presentations simple. Remember that Paul told young Christians in Corinth that they needed the "milk" of the Word before he fed them the "solid food" (see 1 Corinthians 3:2). Ellen White wrote, "Never search for words that will give the impression that you are learned. The greater your simplicity, the better will your words be understood" (*Gospel Workers*, p. 89).

4. Always ask the student if he has a Bible. Help him become familiar with the Bible if he needs some help. Show him the table of contents that will enable him to locate the books of the Old and New Testaments. Show him how the Bible books are divided into chapters and verses. Look up several Bible texts with him to make sure he knows how to do it himself.

5. Accept the student just as he is with all of his problems and difficulties. Do not attempt to change him. Don't preach to him or tell him that something he is doing is wrong. At this point, your role is to be his friend. As he studies the Bible, God will convict him about the things in his life that need to change. If you point your finger and condemn, it will hurt his feelings or make him defensive—and it's very likely he will stop studying. Always remember that it is the role of the Holy Spirit to convict, correct, and reprove (see John 16:5–15). Never assume the role of the Holy Spirit.

Recently I heard about Sarah—a woman who had not been to church for three years because someone had hurt her feelings. A friend had been trying to get Sarah to come back to church, but she kept saying no. Finally, however, Sarah decided to give church another try. On her first Sabbath back in church, a well meaning church member took Sarah aside and began lecturing her about her past behavior—telling her that she shouldn't have stayed away from church fellowship and that now she needed to attend every week. Needless to say, that did not warm Sarah's heart toward that congregation.

Why scold people when Jesus so clearly lays out for us the example of His Father in the parable of the prodigal son? Like the father in that story, run to the individual who is returning. Throw your arms around him. Show your delight in seeing him. Rejoice that he has returned. Forget about what he has done in the past—even if it disappointed you. He's back! Don't build walls; build friendship. Lay out stepping-stones to the church!

This same principle is also vital when it comes to giving Bible studies: "It is always humiliating to have one's errors pointed out. None should make the experience more bitter by needless censure. No one was ever reclaimed by reproach; but many have thus been repelled and have been led to steel their hearts against conviction. A tender spirit, a gentle, winning deportment, may save the erring and hide a multitude of sins" (Ellen G. White, *The Ministry of Healing*, p. 166).

6. Follow the order of the series of study guides. Each study builds on the previous one. You are building on a foundation. Matthew 7:24–27 tells us that we can build on a foundation of rock or upon a foundation of sand. Skipping subjects, or studying the lessons out of order, is like building on sand. When problems and challenges come up for the student, he may fall away because he hasn't been grounded in the Word. Think of climbing a set of stairs. In order to reach the top, don't skip any steps! You might fall and get hurt.

7. You aren't the one actually giving the Bible study—God is. As you study with the student, God is speaking to his heart through His Word. Trust Him to do His work well. Jesus said, " 'Without Me you can do nothing' " (John 15:5).

8. Never "push" or "argue." If you do, all you will accomplish is to build a barrier between you and the student. If you have a difference of opinion with the student regarding a topic, show respect, acceptance, understanding, and kindness. If you answer all questions by the Bible, the student will better be able to reflect on God's Word and listen to the Spirit speaking to his heart. "The Savior knew that no argument, however logical, would melt hard hearts or break through the crust of worldliness and selfishness" (Ellen G. White, *Acts of the Apostles*, p. 31).

9. Do special things for your student. Be a genuine friend. If possible, spend time doing something enjoyable with him.

10. When appropriate, loan the student a book, videos, or DVDs on a topic.

11. If your visit is a "doorstep" visit and you are reviewing the lesson's answers at the door, spend only about five or ten minutes. You can always take the student's completed response sheet or study guide with you to review, mark, and return. This may not be an ideal situation, but it is appropriate.

If the student invites you into the home, spend forty-five minutes to an hour at the most. If it is an organized study with a small group in the home, spend about ninety minutes as an average time. But be sure the group members are comfortable devoting that amount of time to the study.

Remember to respect the time schedule. Leave the student(s) wishing you would stay longer, rather than wishing you would leave sooner! If you leave while they are still interested, they will look forward to your next visit.

12. Cover one study guide per week. This is the schedule that most students feel comfortable with. However, some students prefer to study two lessons each week. But remember: A student can sometimes "overeat" when feeding on the Word. Students need time to "digest" what is brand new to them. That is what Paul was referring to when he spoke about the "milk" and "solid food" of the Scriptures.

13. Do not speak negatively about other churches or their beliefs.

14. Don't ask a student to read a text out loud until you know he is comfortable reading publicly. You don't want to embarrass him.

15. Avoid Adventist jargon—words and terms that are familiar to Adventists but that have little or no meaning to others.

16. Answer all questions using the words of the Bible—not your own opinions, another book, the Spirit of Prophecy, etc. Remember to pray and trust God. Allow God to use you—and be amazed at what He does! "If the worker keeps his heart uplifted in prayer, God will help him to speak the right word at the right time" (Ellen G. White, *Gospel Workers*, p. 120).

Chapter 7

Obtaining Decisions

D o you remember the story I shared at the beginning of this little book—the story of my very first Bible student, Pat? After I reviewed each Bible guide with her, I would ask, "Do you have any questions?"

She usually responded, "No; it's quite clear." Finally we came to the last lesson. I asked, "Do you have any questions?"

"No," she replied. "It's quite clear."

I didn't know what to do next! I hadn't thought to ask anyone how to end a series of Bible studies. I wasn't experienced enough to even realize that I needed to ask someone for help! As a result, I never asked Pat to make a decision about what she had studied. I've learned since what a mistake that was. Generally, a person doesn't go through an entire series of Bible studies and then say, "I accept everything I have been studying. Please baptize me." Now, once in a great while, this does happen. But in my experience, it doesn't happen very often. Usually, people don't make decisions unless you ask them to make decisions. You have to bring them to the point of realizing that they need to do something about what they have studied and learned; that they need to make a decision to accept Jesus Christ and His truth.

Here are some principles that will help you understand the importance of having your Bible students make a decision—and how to cause that to happen.

Decision principle #1. Major life decisions are usually made incrementally. It's difficult to make a major decision all at once. Most people find it much easier to make a series of small decisions. This means that you need to call for a decision at the end of *every* Bible study. Whatever the topic of a particular lesson, lead the student to make a decision to incorporate that truth into his or her life in a practical way. In other words, help them to see that they need to do more than understand what the lesson is teaching; they also need to have it make a difference in their life.

Decision principle #2. Incremental decisions add up to determine the direction a person takes in life. If a person makes a decision regarding the topic of every study guide, then, when they have completed the set of lessons, they will have decided to completely follow Jesus. Over a period of time, decision by decision, they have chosen the spiritual direction of their life.

Decision principle #3. Expect the student to respond positively at the completion of each study guide. If you are hesitant about the student's need to make a decision or if you are reluctant to ask him or her to make a decision, the student will conclude that it's not really important to say yes regarding the truth he or she has studied. On the other hand, if you ask for a decision in a positive, confident manner, letting it arise naturally out of the lesson, the student will likely respond positively.

Decision principle #4. Biblical information that is simply head knowledge and not a heart experience will not benefit the student now nor lead him to eternal life. It's important that the student understand what the Bible says and what the lesson is teaching. But their understanding must be more than just head knowledge, a mere intellectual acceptance. The truth they have learned must touch the heart. Always apply the truth of the lesson to the heart and to our relationship with Jesus. And always ask the student to respond with the heart to what he or she has learned.

Decision principle #5. Usually, a person takes four steps in making a decision. We all follow these four steps in any kind of decision that we make—whether it is a spiritual decision or something as ordinary as buying a car. If you were going to purchase a new car, you would probably go about it like this.

1. You gather *information.* You look at different models and compare features and prices. You clarify any questions that arise in your mind—either by asking someone or by reading or on the Internet. Once

you have all the pertinent information, you move to the next step.

2. You begin feeling *conviction* that you should purchase the car based on the information you have gathered. As the conviction to purchase the car becomes stronger, you move to the next step.

3. You *want* this car! A desire builds within you. You can picture yourself driving the car; you become emotionally involved. And when the desire becomes strong enough, you reach the final step.

4. You *take action* and purchase the car.

The same steps apply when we make decisions about spiritual matters. You need to understand these steps to a decision so that you can help your student through the process as he or she responds to the truths of each lesson.

Decision principle #6. Ask certain questions in order to help the student make a decision about the topic studied in each lesson. The questions to ask are really quite simple:

- Is this topic clear to you? Do you have any questions?
- Would you like to tell Jesus "thank You" for . . . creating the world? . . . the plan He has for your life? . . . the salvation He offers you? . . . the Holy Spirit? Ask this question using the topic of the particular lesson you have just studied. Then pray with the student, thanking God for that particular

truth and asking Him to apply it to your life and to the life of your student.

- When you study the major, testing subjects such as accepting Jesus as Savior or the seventh-day Sabbath, ask, "Have you thought about accepting Jesus as your personal Savior?" "Have you thought about keeping the seventh-day Sabbath?" If the student answers "Yes," then ask, "Would you like to accept Jesus into your life right now?" "Would you like to tell Jesus right now that you intend to keep His seventh-day Sabbath?" If the student hesitates or doesn't seem sure that he or she is ready to make such a commitment, don't push further. Instead, affirm him or her. Say something positive about the student's progress in his or her spiritual journey of discovery in the Word. Then pray with the student that God will continue to guide both you and the student as you continue to study together.

Decision principle #7. Your role is to ask the question; God's role is to convict the heart. Remember, when you ask a person about his or her response to the topic you have studied, it is easier for the student to affirm the general topics that are the subjects of the early lessons. By the time you come to such subjects as accepting Jesus as Savior, you should have built up a relationship with the student; hopefully, you will have become friends because of the quality time you have spent together studying God's Word. It's always easier to ask a friend a personal question than it is to ask a mere acquaintance.

Keep in mind, too, that it's the Holy Spirit's job—not your's—to convict the heart. Your job is simply to ask the questions and make it possible for the Holy Spirit to impress and convict the student's heart. In the end, whether a person makes a positive decision regarding spiritual truth depends on his own response to the Holy Spirit.

Decision principle #8. If a person does not accept Jesus as the Lord and Savior of his life, keep studying with him. Don't assume that he has objections that won't be answered in time. Most sets of Bible study guides provide numerous opportunities for the student to accept Jesus. The Holy Spirit can use even "head knowledge" on various topics to convict the person to accept Christ. The material he keeps learning can gradually help him respond positively and accept Jesus as his Savior.

Decision principle #9. It is usually easier for the student to make a decision if the subject is new and fresh to him. If a person has already become familiar with the truths of the Bible and hasn't made a decision to accept them, it is sometimes more difficult for the Holy Spirit to awaken conviction. That is why it is important to encourage your student to respond in some positive way to each topic as it is presented. A simple decision on a more general truth prepares the student to respond positively to the more difficult decisions that lie ahead. For example, a decision to thank God for the plan of salvation prepares the way for the student to later apply the plan of salvation personally by accepting Jesus as his own Savior from sin.

Decision principle #10. You are God's child. Jesus would have died for you if you were the only person on earth who would accept His sacrifice. God is pleased you are following His command to "Go." As you share His Word with others, relax. The Holy Spirit is the One giving the Bible study and calling for the decision; you are simply His visiting partner!

Chapter 8

The Spirit-Filled Life

Acts chapter 4 is one of my favorite soul-winning passages in the Bible. In this chapter we see Peter and John preaching and giving Bible studies. The things these apostles were saying upset the Jewish rulers, elders, and scribes greatly. The enthusiastic response of the people to the apostles' message annoyed the Jewish leaders. So Annas, the high priest, and other members of the rulers called Peter and John in for a talk. The Bible says, "And when they had set them in the midst, they asked, 'By what power or by what name have you done this?' " (Acts 4:7). Peter responded to their question by giving a wonderful testimony.

What was the result? "Now when they saw the boldness of Peter and John, and perceived that they were uneducated and untrained men, they marveled. And they realized that they had been with Jesus" (verse 13). Still, these religious leaders ordered the apostles to quit teaching about Jesus. But they replied, " 'We cannot but speak the things which we have seen and heard' " (verse 20).

Peter and John continued ministering in Jerusalem and praying with fellow Christians. These are the words that came out of that prayer circle: " 'Now, Lord, look on their threats, and grant to Your servants that with all boldness they may speak Your word, by stretching out Your hand to heal, and that signs and wonders may be done through the name of Your holy Servant Jesus' " (verses 29, 30).

I particularly like what happened at the end of this session of prayer. "And when they had prayed, the place where they were assembled together was shaken; and they were all filled with the Holy Spirit, and they spoke the word of God with boldness" (verse 31).

Remember, these disciples all came from very ordinary backgrounds. They were people just like you and me. They hadn't gone to the religious schools of their day; they weren't trained theologians. But they loved Jesus and had been trained by Him. They wanted to tell others about Him. Like us, they were often scared, nervous, and unsure of themselves. The Bible tells us how they hid for a while in an upper room for fear of the religious authorities! But in spite of their weaknesses, they prayed and relied on the Holy Spirit, and God was able to use them mightily!

Today, God is saying to you, "Go to your friends and neighbors, go to the people you work with. Go— and guess what? I will be with you. I will make you successful in winning souls. I will speak through you with boldness! Go! I am with you until the end of the world."

Are you ready? Let's go and share Jesus with those who need to know Him and His truth!